mac's year

1988

Cartoons from the Daily Mail

Stan McMurtry **mac**

Published by Harmsworth Publications Ltd., for
Mail Newspapers p.l.c.
London EC4 Y0JA

ISBN 0 85144 463 6

Printed in Great Britain by
Spottiswoode Ballantyne Ltd., Colchester and London.

"That's strange ladies — Senor Kenneth Clarke was here a minute ago ..."

"... and do you, Nicholas Robinson, because of the current inexplicable bachelor boom, take this woman on a timeshare basis for the last fortnight in August each year ...?"

"Here's your comfy cell, Englishman - it's got TV, hot water, flush toilets, ping-pong and Jaques the Belgian strangler"

"Well, Telecom's new chairman has made a fantastic start to improving it's public image!"

SEPTEMBER 14

"Well shucks, if you were new to Arizona would you want to be cooped up in a darned Popemobile all day?"

"We want you to have a better life than we've had, son - so we've put your name down for a private prison"

SEPTEMBER 18

"Oh yes, he loved his first day - just one small thing . . . your use of super glue . . ."

"Arthur, there's a Chief Constable Anderton to see you about a new edition to the disciplinary code . . ."

"Fantastic idea! Next time she comes up here hunting - make like a snake!"

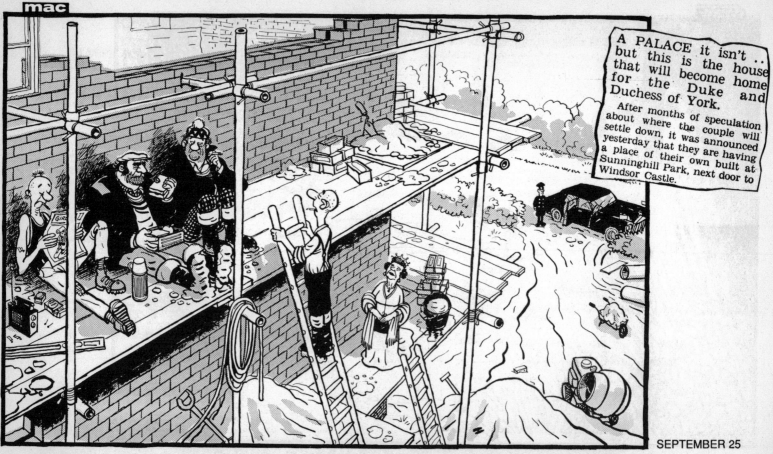

SEPTEMBER 25

"I said you was 'avin your lunch, Nobby, but there's somebody wants a quote for a bit of building
work over at Windsor . . ."

"No, this room you'll end up in isn't a gas chamber . . . it's . . . it's, yes, it's a padded cell in a psychiatric hospital"

"Bad news I'm afraid. Apparently it's four months for Keith Best, four months for Keith Lander Best, four months for . . ."

"False alarm! The man with the gun at the amusement arcade was only trying to win a coconut"

"Sorry Galini, but since the Government's crackdown on knives you're not pulling in the crowds any more"

"He can go back hame the noo - they've called off the hunt"

"... then should you take part in any further criminal activities, it bleeps us and you've got three seconds before it explodes"

"Good news, Norman! The electricity is back on, the TV's working and Michael Fish says there's going to be a heatwave . . ."

THE Prince and Princess of Wales remained 500 miles apart yesterday.

Increasingly leading separate lives they are thought to have seen each other only once in the past month.

OCTOBER 20

"It's either Princess Diana arriving for a reunion with Charles or the Royal Navy trying for a reunion with Andrew"

"Not wishing to be unsympathetic, sonny, but one more bleat about having to sell your Porsche and guess where we'll shove your Filofax?"

"Remember the old days when they would just shake people's hands?"

OCTOBER 23

"Well, well Sarge. I wonder who the change of clothes and getaway horse was intended for?"

"It's the vicar dear - he's come to give us a moral lead . . ."

MRS THATCHER has launched a bitter attack on the Archbishop of Canterbury and other Church leaders for failing to give the nation a moral lead.

OCTOBER 27

mac

TV shows beam in on the royal marriage

OCTOBER 28

"We've tried to ensure your privacy was not disturbed, sir. But the First Battalion of the Queen's Marriage Councellors has breached the walls . . ."

IT was one of those unforgettable summer mornings at historic Bratton Court.

The first rays of dawn shone through the mullioned windows. From the panelled hall echoed the strains .of Beethoven's Fifth. And in the courtyard, the Hon. Roland Lytton was smashing two Land-Rovers together, again and again.

For two hours the lovelorn aristocrat farmer drove his reinforced steel vehicle into that of his rival Tom Lister, reducing it to a mass of twisted metal.

As for Lister, a windsurf board salesman, he remained upstairs in a drunken stupor, sharing a bed with Lytton's girlfriend Julie Croker.

OCTOBER 30

"Good morning, Sir, I see that since you wrecked his Land-Rover your young rival has acquired another vehicle . . ."

NOVEMBER 4

"... 5.16p per unit plus standing charge £6.37 plus 10% to help Energy Minister
with increased child maintenance payments ..."

"Aw gee, Mr President — the whole world is waiting for a slightly more positive kinda move!"

LEST WE FORGET — what heartless, murdering scum the IRA are

"Guess what, dear? Little Ronnie has been dabbling in the Stock Exchange"

NOVEMBER 10

"Come on, Mavis, own up - is it true that Danny La Rue has proposed"

"I'm sorry, Shirley — your intended has run off with the vicar!"

NOVEMBER 13

"Filthy and unhygienic, eh? — SEIZE, ROVER!"

"... so come on you English boys, lay down your arms, you know you can't win ..."

"The worst Elton would do it you were playing badly was put you in the reserves ..."

"They say that back in the 1980s this used to be the North Sea"

"See? That wasn't too painful an extraction - now let's have a look at your teeth"

NOVEMBER 30

"Look dear, if it will ease the burden a little, I'm quite happy to go without Christmas pudding this year"

"Oh, that's the new Iran Tunnel, M'sieur — so their bombers can come and go as they please"

"Right, team. This is a map showing the locations of the new unvandalised
Mercury telephone boxes . . ."

DECEMBER 2

DECEMBER 4

"It's Runcie again — his order for fire, flood, pestilence and locusts hasn't arrived at Crockfords Directory yet"

"Stop moaning, Denis. D'you want Reagan and Gorbachev's other halves to steal all the fashion limelight?"

mac

TWO simple signatures — and history is made.

With delighted smiles, President Reagan and Soviet leader Mikhail Gorbachev formally completed the treaty scrapping 2,800 nuclear missiles.

DECEMBER 8

"Okay, before we start — have you heard the one about the thick Russian, the elephant and the banana sandwich?"

"Excuse me, madam, would you see me across the road? I'm reserve umpire"

DECEMBER 12

BRITISH CALEDONIAN boss Sir Adam Thomson gave British Airways chairman Lord King a 'hands off' warning last night in the battle to take over his airline.

Sir Adam accused Lord King of operating a 'dirty tricks' department to thwart a rival bid for a major slice of B-Cal by the Scandinavian airline SAS

DECEMBER 14

"Looks like the Scandinavian bid has been accepted — here come the flight crew"

"I think Mrs Anderton has overcooked the potatoes again"

DECEMBER 15

"Y'know Mike — all things considered — I think this time if the umpire or his assistant say 'Out' I'll take their word for it"

DECEMBER 21

"Come on, Mr Pilbean, cheer up! Ish Chrishtmas, the Govmentsh shaking up the N.H.S.
We can do your operation at last!"

mac

THE KING'S HEAD

NEXT PUB DOWN THE ROAD

EDWINA CURRIE'S message to drinkers at a pub opening was unequivocal.

'Many people believe it's okay to have a pint or so if they are driving but it's far more sensible to stick to soft drinks,' declared the Junior Health Minister.

Her husband Ray, who had just downed two pints of bitter, then drove her home.

DECEMBER 22

"Since that one slip-up, looks like Edwina's trying her best to set a good example ..."

"... The BBC has apologised to the Queen and Mr Cole has been moved to another department"

DECEMBER 23

JANUARY 19

"I think I preferred things when Edward was in the Marines"

JANUARY 20

"Sorry I'm late dear — dropped into the Rose and Crown for a pint, had a game of darts with the girls — what's for supper?"

"Arthur dear, have you given any thought to what you'll do if you lose the presidential election?"

"Sorry, Ma'am, flying is fine, skiing, horse riding and canoeing are dodgy, but a Tyson fight is definitely out"

"For heaven's sake! I'll be alright, I tell you!"

FEBRUARY 3

"At least it's given us people from the contageous disease isolation ward a chance to get up and about"

FEBRUARY 5, 1988

"Oh, come come sergeant. You have accused this young lady of grievous bodily harm by punching you on the nose - you look alright to me . . ."

CS gas thrown by Sibson title fight thugs

TWO CS gas canisters were thrown as crowd violence rocked another world boxing title fight last night.

FEBRUARY 9

" . . . and a wonderful left hook almost got past his riot gear . . . then a right to the gas mask . . ."

GOVERNMENT minister John Gummer made a withering attack yesterday on the failures of moral leadership of the Church of England in general, and the Archbishop of York in particular.

FEBRUARY 10

"Shouldn't you be up there calling for chastity and fidelity like John Gummer suggests, vicar?"

FEBRUARY 12

"Well you should have warned me before you went to Brussels. I thought it was just the House of Commons they've been allowed to take the cameras into . . ."

mac

ELI LILLY
OPREN

In a major step forward for the Opren campaign, Health Minister Tony Newton yesterday agreed to consider pressing drugs giant Eli Lilly to set up a multi-million pound trust fund for thousands of victims.

FEBRUARY 16, 1988

"No it's not sunlight the boss is sensitive to - more like world criticism"

SQUADS of 'pirate' Australian television technicians were preparing to fly into Britain last night in a dramatic move which could black out ITV screens nationwide.

TV-am chief Bruce Gyngell plans to call in the crews to take over at the beleaguered breakfast station after sacking his own technicians, who have been locked out for two months in a dispute over working practices.

FEBRUARY 19

"Anne Diamond's going to be livid if her Australian replacement pushes the ratings up"

FEBRUARY 22

"Sacre bleu! Not again! Shouldn't you be at home making tea for M'sieu Lloyd-Webber?"

"Incompetent idiots! Look Doris — another near miss!"

mac

ENERGY Secretary Cecil Parkinson yesterday launched the world's biggest sell-off with his plans to break up the £27billion electricity industry.

FEBRUARY 26

"The Electricity Board says the bathroom, the upstairs loo and one socket in the hall are all on separate grids now and we'll have to apply for reconnection with the new authorities."

"Hope you've raised the drawbridge, Soames — here come the first batch of Leap Year proposals, clutching their lists of millionaires."

"Bless him. Our Kevin's never forgotten the sacrifices we made to give him
a private education ..."

MICHAEL Jackson may be dropped from Pepsi's multi-million dollar British TV advertising campaign because of a backroom row.

MARCH 4

"It's Michael Jackson again doc — he got so upset that the British won't see him in TV ads, all his old stitches came undone"

"At this point, Hawkins, you explain to the gentleman there's an amnesty for drunken drivers and say how awfully pleased we'd be if he'd come back to our hospitality room for a cup of coffee"

"I didn't know what was going on, just did my job — but I admit I had a sneaky suspicion what Waldheim was up to ..."

MRS THATCHER lay siege yesterday to the last urban citadels of socialism.

She revealed a dynamic £3 billion plan to bring new life to Britain's run-down inner cities.

MARCH 9

"Don't disturb your father — he's planning where to put the jacuzzi and cocktail bar."

THE good men of Sherwood Forest fired an arrow into the air yesterday and killed off a slice of romance.

The love story of outlaw Robin Hood and Maid Marian was a myth, a lot of nonsense, said the city fathers of Nottingham.

MARCH 11

"Aw, don't sulk, sweetie, the scribe feels that it would look better in the history books if you changed your name to Maid Marian . . ."

"You'd think he would've told her what he was putting in his Budget wouldn't you?"

MARRIAGE is an honourable institution — and that's official at last.

After years of debating the way husbands and wives are jointly taxed, and bemoaning the fact that couples who live in sin get all the tax breaks, the Government has confirmed its commitment to marriage in a major reform of family taxation to come into effect in 1990.

MARCH 16

"I tell you it's still cheaper to live together till 1990, Doris!"

"Strewth, Marge! You sat next to Ian Botham on the plane and you didn't get his autograph?"

"It says here that today's woman is for faithfulness and the death penalty — and would like to run her own business — a bit like your wife really, Mr Wilkins ..."

"No sir, I have not been drinking! There's a dinosaur at the gate waving a Union Jack, pulling it's forelock and grovelling ...!"

mac

CRUSADE FOR SOCIALISM

L

BENN & HEFFER LEADERSHIP CRUSADE

THE Hard Left is to hurl Labour into a damaging leadership battle.

The nightmare ticket of Anthony Wedgwood Benn and Eric Heffer agreed last night to challenge Neil Kinnock and his deputy Roy Hattersley for their jobs.

MARCH 25

"This may take some time — the horse has died laughing"

"I warned you not to get too close! This animal's in training for going over the Alps with Ian Botham."

"I am sorry, Denis! I thought it was Lawson trying a coup d'etat!"

THE union stranglehold on TV and film-making is facing its most searching inquiry.

Ministers yesterday ordered the Monopolies Commission to investigate the industries — Mrs Thatcher's toughest move yet against what she regards as the last bastion of over-mighty union-power.

MARCH 30

"Good evening. Our guest tonight is from the Monopolies Commission, who are investigating overmanning in the TV industry ..."

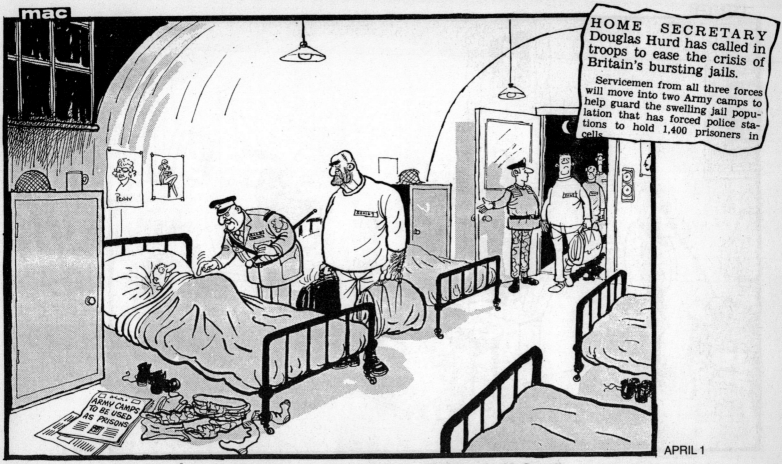

"Shove up a bit, Private Conway — you're sharing with Strangler McGrew"

"Oh yes. Very quiet and restful, thank you — I've been reading and Maggie's been doing some ...
er ... needlework."

"They've decided to go back to tried and tested methods — like when Michael Fish's bunion aches it'll rain"

"Nice shot, Bruce, but I think the Sheila you just stopped sneakin' in through the gate
with your boomerang is the lady we're supposed to be guarding ..."

"... slow down a bit! Mind that bike ... right, turn left ... watch out for that old lady ...!"

APRIL 19

"Before considering your verdict I strongly advise members of the jury to disregard these ridiculous claims in the Press about corrupt lawyers"

"Don't tell me you fell for that 'You're not a traffic warden, you're Jerry Hall doing a sexy advert' routine again?"

"Oh, stop moaning, Ron — what else did you think 'Suspended for a month' meant?"

"This way, Sir - foot down, 80 mph up the ramp, over the pickets, and welcome to P & O Ferries"

"I suppose you took on who you could, but tell the new bosun it's not quite the same as dinghy sailing"

"Get over to Holland quickly! It's bound to be the British soldier's fault."

"Slow down a little, Gerald. I think you've been spotted by one of those 'Spy in the sky' speed traps ..."

POLICE protection has been offered to 28 peers after death threats by activists demanding changes to the Government's controversial legislation on homosexuality.

MAY 4

"Don't you think you're overreacting, Rupert dear? — he'll probably only come at you with his handbag."

"The choice is yours, lads — either join us here for weeks of union solidarity, or stay on Canberra and blackleg your way round the exotic sunspots of the world ... lads?"

"May I suggest to the happy couple that the book advocating good rows for healthy marriages was referring to a little later in the relationship?"

"It gets worse! — Look what a fool Reagan makes of himself next week!"

"I don't know! The Government spends £10 million on improving the zoo and you're still moaning!"

"From what I can gather we appear to have won some vulgar football cup or something ..."

"There go another two who need glasses, Sarge."

"Are you sure this is Neighbours?"

"Mr Fieldmouse, sir! That patient left five minutes ago ..."

"Now that my honourable colleague's wife has checked the place for loose women, will he ask her to wait outside?"

"Apparently while we were doon at Wembley, faither was listening tae Mrs Thatcher preachin' aboot a return to discipline, morals and traditional family values ..."

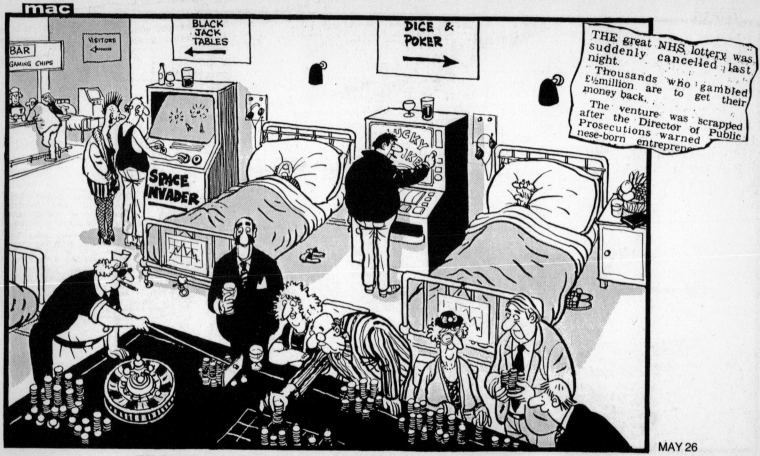

"Well, nobody told me they'd cancelled the N.H.S. lottery idea"

"Does this mean that her father won't be coming to Parents' Day?"

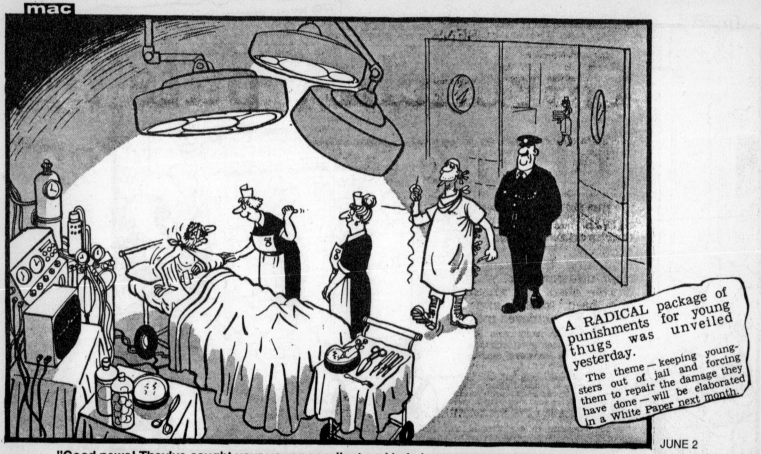

"Good news! They've caught your young assailant and he's been sentenced to repair the damage he did"

"Excuse me, sweetie, I think we've got our first protest about Tumbledown Two"

JUNE 9

"I can't hang you, but by heaven you'll serve 20 years in a cell with only a black-and-white TV and ping-pong restricted to every other Thursday!"

By JOHN WELLINGTON

BARBARA Woodhouse, beloved by animals and their owners the world over, died yesterday at the age of 78.

mac

JULY 11

"It <u>was</u> heaven. Rolling in dirt, barking and fighting and doing as we pleased — then Barbara Woodhouse came up ..."

"Did you book a call to a Mrs Thatcher?"

"I said, anyone who queues for 24 hours at an airport for a foreign holiday needs his head examined"

"What d'you mean you let him go? - We told you to shoot him"

JULY 19

**"There go the Russians who are checking our missile numbers at the base — give 'em
a friendly wave you guys ..."**

"Here is the news — European Commissioner Leon Brittan has just announced that VAT will be trebled on luxury yachts, mooring charges and yacht accessories ..."

"Guess what, dear? - I've gone into business"

"Don't talk about the drug syndicate — There's a rumour that this Moynihan guy had
an accomplice ..."

"Isn't it romantic? In return Charles is giving Diana a whole seven-hour epic of him talking to a geranium ..."

"Stop moaning, dear, over here nobody would ever mess with Crocodile Dundenis"

"I'm sorry Peasmold, the barracks are full — you'll have to find room for two more ..."

COMEDIAN Ken Dodd's passport was seized yesterday after a claim that he might flee the country to avoid a tax fraud trial. The self-styled Squire of Knotty Ash faces 27...

COURTS 1–10

AUGUST 12

"I believe Ponsonby-Smythe is rather keen to be given the Ken Dodd case ..."

"Oh, just a few staff changes for when I leave. Anyway, good luck, George - you have my full confidence . . ."

"Neil's very busy getting the garage ready for the Labour Party conference in October ..."

"So when I sat down and worked out just how much the new British Rail season tickets
were going to cost ..."

"Remember, Carol dear, this is only until your ratings go up"

"For 14 years I've endured his varicose veins, his marital problems and his only joke ...
but that was lunchtimes and evenings only ...!"

"First things first, professor — is it safe for my wife to wear her seal-skin coat?"